FATBERGS
ANDREA
MBARUSHIMANA

KFS
PAMPHLETS

Newton-le-Willows

Published in the United Kingdom in 2021
by The Knives Forks And Spoons Press,
51 Pipit Avenue,
Newton-le-Willows,
Merseyside,
WA12 9RG.

ISBN 978-1-912211-80-7

Acknowledgements:

'The Hoodie', p.19, was published in *Anthology 1. Light*, by The Black Light Engine Driver Press, December 2020.

'Signage', p.27, was published in *The Curlew, Vol III, Issue II, Crataegus*, March 2019

Thank you to all the Cov poets (and environs), for inspiration and support; especially Anthony Owen, for introducing me to KFS and Aysar Ghassan – my go-to reader

Thank you Alec at KFS for bringing *Fatbergs* into the light.

'Maria' was written in response to a prompt by Luke Kennard in '52' from Nine Arches Press, Jo Bell and guest poets, 2015. I actually did go to the desert though!

Supported using public funding by
ARTS COUNCIL ENGLAND

LOTTERY FUNDED

Love and thanks to JP (my Peter) and Safi

Contents

Charlemaigne Decides

Time is a single grey hair in the bathroom mirror.
Then another. And another.
We exist apart from each other –
in a snow-globe, maybe,
somewhere far from air or sun.
Outside a life time stretches, supine.

We congregate at safe distances,
loins filling with sap.
Spring, don't leave us curdling,
hung and drawn in shadowed living quarters.

The people who lived through year Zero were clueless.
Christ? Who was he? Through the window
we watch another lonely martyr.

Virtual Reality

I treat my body like a skin and bone avatar
maintained by a server somewhere beyond my interest.
How do I look right now?
I just made my own face.

The bird on the fence sees me and lifts its head.
Take the photo to the server.
My head opening like a meat flower.
Come to me for carrion.

No sooner born,
the first insult my daughter learns is *noob*
(thumbs clicking as she lays out *bacon hairs*)
the second insult she learns is *Boomer.*

We are all worms in a server somewhere.
Cascading our behemoth bodies through a pixel town
on the prowl for younger versions of ourselves to eat.
This is a manageable definition of success.

Motherhood

… is a mechanical phase.
Goes on and on
past imagination.
You become all lead and foil.
A behemoth of gradual accretion.
People come along and pick bits off,
or follow behind collecting the bits that fall.
You try to keep it together, soft stuff on the inside
so as not to release a tidal wave,
but every step feels perilous.
Look in the mirror:
you are an ecosystem,
a set of parentheses.

Andrea Mbarushimana

Zero Hour

People always ask: "What happened and where were you
and what did it feel like?"
I was alone at the kitchen table,
kids in the living room,
husband upstairs,
my left hand warm around a coffee cup.

I was sat at the chicken table,
lids in the kiving room,
hus-stairs upland,
a strange creature hatched out of my chest,
like a nalian.
It ran on needle legs.
It legged on it's needles, towards my joat, my thraw line,
leaving it's trail of acid blooming like a hot flower
through my sternum.

Four days later I was back at the same table,
in the chame snair.
Everything was the same and
Everything was different.

Jetsam

The time we sat on your bed
watching you wheeze, your big eyes rolling back,
lashes beating like wings trying to take off from a lake.
The Doctor said to let "nature take it's course,"
Instead, we took your life in our hands and carried it to hospital
like a broken swallow.

Or that time in A&E we sneaked in the Baileys you'd asked for,
decanted into ginger beer cans, giggling like idiots.
We thought that was the end,
until – asleep – you sat up in bed and said:
"You can't take me now, I'm not ready yet."

Both those times I was thinking 'Where? and Now?'
And 'how did it fall to us to row the boat –
who didn't know port from starboard?'

My earliest memory is a nightmare
of falling into the toilet,
being swallowed up,
unreachable, alone.

"Where does the toilet go Daddy?
Because I don't think it's heaven."

Andrea Mbarushimana

Cheyne-Stokes

The mechanical spasm of his chest
is slowly juddering down.
Light tiptoes through the door ...

... breath in / breath out ...

Love is a verb. She plays it
to an audience of herself,
a gentle hand across his brow,
a sponge dabbing black lips ...

... breath in / breath out ...

mist fills the room.
She whispers words learnt from his mouth.
Honeyed, they bloom
petals reaching for moonlight ...

... breath in / breath out ...

Death's made himself comfy
in the one spare plastic seat.
What can we do?
We welcome him,
settle into his company ...

... breath in / breath out ...

Headlights make their passage across the ceiling.
The day's setting itself in amber.
We wait in the chill room for hours and hours, we wait ...

... breath in / breath out ...
... breath in / breath out ...
... breath in / breath out ...

Socially Distanced

Outside the Care Home
your stuff was piled under an awning.

Heaving it into the car boot, I remember
the time Dad posted me a box of Coventry air –
he had his ups and downs before the end.

These boxes are all disappointingly toothless:
Dad's pencil stubs and dust bunnies,
your May tinsel.

When I go what will I leave behind?
I wonder, do pressed nettle leaves
retain their sting?

Apology

Sorry I took the smile
you left in the cold air.
I hung it on the nearest autumn tree
haemorrhaging leaves
like promises.
It was so sweet it turned my teeth to ice.

St Theresa of Avila

Priests take out their pieces of cadaver and
inhale the stink of sanctity they say she smelt
of, even before death.
That stench of wasted womanhood,
that Godliness.
Imagine purity that isn't soapy, cotton fresh,
a base note tanged with blood.

Men all over Europe hunker over body parts
that were untouched while turgid, pinked and pert:
Father Gracian takes her little finger, strokes, prays fervently;
Lisbon her hand; Ronda her left eyeball.
At Alba de Tormes they have her heart,
despite her insistence it belonged to the Almighty.

Each night of her life she was speared by angels in dream
viscera floating round her like a halo,
And in the morning she would levitate.
Her fellow nuns, embarrassed, clutched her skirts
trying to bring her down.

Gisozi

Yesterday's heron shrieks the end of sleep
right through my skull –
all spiny barbs waiting to soften into feathers.
A house-girl making breakfast.
Noses blow dust, taste smoked in eucalyptus.
We count mosquito bites, eat bread that's toasted
on the plate, while we wait.
The fizz of welding across the street has stopped.
Strange birds hide in the copse where the brick man stacks his bricks
among trees that count their lifespan in dawn choruses.
A tiny lizard escapes from my daughter's shoe,
and rhythmic church song hypnotises a congregation down the street.
We rise through air like soup, using the short cut.
There's a breeze up here that bends the trees to gossip.
Down across waste-ground, turn right
past the battle of the band widths, past the data shacks,
the track stops, Chez Venant –
her mansion built on helping couples with their sex lives.
When we get back from the bar – brochettes and consequences –
he's still making bricks,
hoeing the clay,
patting it into the same mould,
stacking them up.
Later when it rains the whole tower vanishes.

Thank God We Never Had Kids

My words, stray hairs I tried to plait into a rope
in order to escape around the u-bend.

You just standing, silent and unresponsive as lard.

Us, a build-up of non-biodegradable material
forming a congealed mass:
skin cells rubbed from all the places you'd touched,
lottery tickets – desperately scratched,
hair from the pillow you'd shed in clumps,
used / unused condoms,
your kidney stones, my ear wax,
your abominable toenails.
All of it forming a golem of fat.
The magic words to animate it spelt out
on it's forehead in our tangled pubes.

I can see it staggering up out of the toilet into the light.
Sending the bare bulb of the bathroom swinging,

yelling: "Mum! Dad!"

Andrea Mbarushimana

Tooth and Claw

The sound system sends your ear drums
pulsing like sewer blobs.
Soft tissues bruise like avocadoes.
Light loses it's way
in the bottom of your shot glass.

Look at the girl with the water-weed hair,
fish-scale sequins glinting,
an eel on the dancefloor.
She wriggles across ground
to a pile of coats upstairs.

Jenny Greenteeth
reeling you in
Nelly Longarms.

She welcomes your rubbish lines
with an otter sharp grin
and when the music crescendos
she'll vomit what's left of you – hair and bone
back up again.

On Instagram she's known as Carmen Winstead –
lures children into wells
to drown themselves, filmed by their friends.

The Hoodie

Is a huge black shape against the wardrobe door.
A maw in the base of an old tree.
A sewer.
I turn away from it.
Stickers shaped like stars fluoresce
Orion's Belt on the side of the bedside table.

I try not to look at you in the morning.
Waves enter your eye and are refracted
within the iris. It glows
gold and amber and leaves your iris
entering mine, burning.
Not yet.

Light cut into ribbons drapes itself across the bed,
spreads in a pattern of interference.
A wave that builds.
A wave that rinses me out onto the floor
on it's way back through the window. It pours
like a prayer from the lips of every doorway as they open
one by one to the morning.

I dress in shadows made of light.
I choose to see you.

Andrea Mbarushimana

Rain

Granite city, light swum shapes
shoaling the walls
I'm walking out of the door again
fish guts damping my nostrils
holding on so hard that
everything is warped
rooms so full of corners
to push into, rooms
so full of walls to punch
crusted, frozen ocean
creeping over sand
trying to stay solid

Concrete city
blackout blind
pin pricked
light ribboning
You, slick second skin
Drops form and swim and sing
between us, there's no weathering
only the weather
Above us blooms
a ceiling rose
I'm vapour

Affection

The Dog comes begging for attention from the
stranger who

calculates risk
(heavy jaw, long yellow teeth, chain tethered, sad eyed),
pauses, offers a hand to sniff.

Encouraged, strokes under
the chin, the collar, to a brief wag.

Scrubs behind the ears.

The dog begins to shake.
"Too much!"
it says,
"Kick me, so I can bite."

Breaking Bad

A continent away
(that feels like another lifetime)
you taught me yoga, meditation.
White robes billowing round twiglet legs
like an upturned lotus.

In the 1930's the people of New York
thought that alligators would make useful pets.

How did you go from that bearded Yogi
to this suited man in the newspaper,
PA to the world's most notorious warlord?

A manhole cover somewhere near Central Park
begins to tremble.

Maria

When I reached the edge of the desert I saw that I was on the Moon and not, as I'd previously believed, in North Africa. You told me where to go, triangulating our position using distant mountains I couldn't understand the significance of. It was as if I was actually still a child. Without you I might not make it.

Mare Cognitum – Sea of Knowledge

Mare Ingenii – Sea of Cleverness

When I reached the middle of the desert I saw a scorpion climb out of my boot. You told me you were Berber, not Arab – as I'd previously thought. I couldn't understand a lot of what you said – my French being awful and my Arabic worse. It was as if I'd attended all the wrong classes at school. Without you I might not have realised.

Mare Marginis – Sea of the Edge

Mare Imbrium – Sea of Showers

When I reached the middle of the desert I saw fossils of oceanic creatures shoaling on a sand sea. You told me the wooden box on your back was for reaching higher, higher. The desert is short on toilets and I couldn't find a bush to hide behind, so I waited until all the other walkers were distant boats floating across a mirror. Without you I felt like a turtle without my shell.

Mare Crisium – Sea of Crises

Mare Nectaris – Sea of Nectar

When I reached the edge of the desert I saw a nightclub. You told me the people standing at the bar were your friends, their names and occupations. But it was the first time I'd seen your hair and I couldn't think about anything else. It was as if I'd never seen hair before. The texture of it under the lights made me crave to touch it. Without you I would never have understood the power of headscarves.

Lost Things

When my mind is still
you float to the surface like a bloated corpse.

There was a time when I would smile into the mirror
and see your face smiling back.

On a collision course with the inevitable
time left a trail of splinters like a dirty snowball
melting down my neck.

This Morning

This morning there were smiles and hellos.
These days I am so gratified by so little kindness
I can't bring myself to be ashamed of it anymore.
If I can find happiness in a ...
whatever ...

This morning it rained so hard.
I remember Rwandans proudly telling me
how it was raining
cats and dogs,
and me saying no one really uses that expression anymore,
when I should've just been impressed.
And I was! Why couldn't I just ... ?
but that is me all over – so precise ...
why can't I be more ... ?

This morning I walked past a man playing
a piece of white pipe like a flute,
lost in his own pied-piper-universe.

This morning I stopped to watch
goldfinches tear the grass
like bloody clowns.

This morning I visited a family
who said their child was ill.
I could see lost people and towns
in their eyes, realised it was one of those times
they needed him near to feel safe.

This morning I crossed a line,
but what line I can't precisely say.

Andrea Mbarushimana

Invitation

come near me

far away

long for the way

I'm short with you

you are a rainbow

of oil on tarmac outside my house

a September carol

I can't stand to be

your ovation

your silence

ringing

walk into my

folded arms

fill my

closed eyes

without you I am

me

Signage

Light slakes frozen branches.
A warning call chipping away at the cradling hum of traffic.

Branches, light-swallowing thickets.

Does a winter tree still feed on sun?
Or do trees also retreat?

Flat panes of yellow leaves dancing.

Time decides which limbs will thicken,
which route to take …
just … bifurcate!
None of this –
tangled thoughts fingering into imagined futures –
am I brave?

Branches,
arrows of branches,
pointing the way.

Flotsam

She'd been in the water a long time. Layers of skin had separated and peeled back. Her torso was fish-nipped, invaded and swollen. Head, arms and legs, all lost and forgotten, had taken other paths through the deep.

Canoe surfing is hard. Just making it through the breakers is like being hit in the face and chest by a succession of small cars. I'd had enough and I was dragging my boat up the sand, when Mark came running over to tell us about the body. After listening to his description I decided not to go over and have a look.

Head, arms and legs, all lost and forgotten, had taken other paths through the deep. Her torso was fish-nipped, invaded and swollen. Layers of her skin separated and peeled back. She'd been in the water a long time.

Coronavirus Coventry

In Llandudno goats spill onto the streets.
The wild boar of Bergamo are leading their piglets through the town.
The whole world is charmed.

Police disperse a group of men
for not standing the requisite 2 metres apart.
Tanked-up, tank-topped,
they run, hooves and howling, past our house.

At the weekend the government announces the end of homelessness.

Jackdaws strut, owning the pavements.
Dealers and alkies trail their entrails all over East Street.
But, with no chicken frying
what will corvids eat?

A friend is jump-scared by feral squirrels near the Cathedral.

Andrea Mbarushimana

Shed Game

No boys allowed all summer long.
We shut the door.
Motes of dust dance through the gloom.
Cobwebs spin and filament
light through disturbed air.
Whispers, giggling.
Small fingers run along the dusty blades
of spades, the tines of forks.
The scent of over-ripe apples
ferments under the tongue.
And touch, as lasered as that
light, strings out along the silks,
sends pleasure shivering
through sun charmed limbs.

Big school now. The pressure of it
sits, begins to settle.
Fat spiders move in from the corners of the shed,
spin summer in a brittle shroud,
straightjacketed,
web over clinging web.

Keeping Up Appearances

In company he shapes his words like syringes,
depositing his poison just under the skin.
A sharp scratch, then a burning.
No one else notices.

It makes her think of Mum.
Bottles of bonhomie that grew
into teetering glass castles all over the house.
Light looks different through that liquored lens:
what was beautiful is bent.

There is an urban legend of a woman who came back
from holiday and at a dinner party
hatched a million baby spiders from her open mouth.

Morning After

Flame of last night fills your mouth with ash.
In the bathroom you stare into the cup.
The law of the toothbrush dictates
each person must use a different colour.
Observe the single available brush, upright
to prevent standing water sitting around it's head.

Vapourising toilet water
may cover the unprotected toothbrush with bacteria.
Consider a pasted finger?
Last night smears into consciousness.
Exchange of bacteria already numbering millions.
Stick to plan A - borrow, wash.

The welcome mat of your tongue is scuffed.
Do not wake the sleeping up!
Leave with your mouth at least
feeling
clean.

Fresh Air

We're sitting on the sofa
limp bodied, woken too early,
frothing our distress in front of the news.

As nature pushes fresh fingers through the letter box
we find ourselves leaning towards the window
only to suck back in, scalded by sun.

Then for one hour each day we are loosened on the world:
advancing metre by metre,
fluorescing over details that last week were so banal –
snails out of hibernation.

Andrea Mbarushimana

Bird Heart

Last night I dreamed I held my heart in my hands
like the pigeon I'd scooped from the drowned sand pit:
a thrumming clag-quilled mess of bone and fibre that used to fly.
I'd set it on a slab of sun to dry

I laugh about it now –
the fact I used to think my heart was tame,
a trained hawk: I'd show it prey,
and after it would sit on my sleeve,
hooded, obedient.

Now I wonder, is my heart that broken pigeon
the baddest boy in school brought to my door?
The boy that every teacher loathed
in hands I'd only ever seen in fists before?

Strange and tender hands
put my heart back in my palms and said
fix this?

Magpie

Nice girls don't fall for magpies.
He strutted across her path
and she threw out all the colours in her wardrobe:
wore the stain of him like a bruise.

She built a nest for the two of them and waited.
Warblers chuckled her name through leaf-light,
dunnock tutted through windows.

Slowly she became the villain in fledgeling tales.
Surrogate mother of cuckoos.
Fed nightmares
while others chanted *bone thief, chick taker.*
She swooned
under the fickle oil-slick of his wing.
Felt his eggs growing inside.
Knew that they would kill her.

Andrea Mbarushimana

Water

It's thirty degrees in the shade.
Your hands squeeze for ripeness,
but I'm so green, I asked my Mum if I was ready.

It's thirty degrees in the shade
and we become anemones
tasting with our fingers.

When you move away
the absence makes me gasp.
You hoist your trousers on,
determined, stomp out of the room,

and come back with water –
two one litre bottles.

As we begin again
you pour the first, fridge cold,
all over us. Shrieks and laughter
shed worries like droplets.

Water squeaks between us.
We are soaking into each other,
soaking into the life-raft-mattress.

The second bottle, we drink.

Strokes

My Grandad taught me to wash brushes
in the palm of my hand:
bristled pets to stroke – squirrel or swine.

When I run them under the tap
colour explodes into the sink,
colour the brush kept secret from the canvas.

I imagine myself, troglobite,
saucer eyed under the down pipe
waiting for rainbows.

Andrea Mbarushimana

The Effect of Increasing Temperature on Organic and Inorganic Nitrogen Reduction in Peat Ecosystems

On top of the haar-kissed mountain
forked-light-oxidised-nitrogen is sucked
into hungry mouths of heather.
Peat cores are cut,
slip through numbed hands and rise
sludge rainbows from the hillside;
black peat,
grey minerals leached out,
a thread of orange iron oxide
and down, and down.

Back in the lab,
warm the cores.
Injecting the trapped breath of bacteria
into the spectrometer –
the book of hillside opens,
reads a prescient elegy
from palpitating carbon heart to arteries of worms.
Nitrogen, too much, like junk food force fed infants.

Twenty years have passed.
I heard a complaint online – where are the voices of scientists?
Where is the research? Gathering dust –
The articles that went unread are written on hills now,
their litmus colour changing.
Mercury climbs and climbs and life runs quicker down the wrong fork in the river –
cataract calling.

Sin Eaters

Under the scum of the surface, the water runs fast.
Spit is a tear salting my mouth.
Wash your Mother's kisses from your face.

Nellies cold fingers grasp, the black stone slips.
We count the seconds as she pulls you down
and run back home, mouths full of fists.

What is right and wrong?
They are memes that move between meanings.
Right is someone falling, sound-tracked by laughter.
Wrong is someone falling with music that makes you feel sad.
Morality is two banks of the same river.

Everyone knows the only way
to teach a girl to swim
is to lead her by the hand until she is out of her depth,
and drink the water she drowns in.

Whelk-Light

A huge whelk, like an old toenail, sits on the window ledge. Light through a ragged hole in the top makes the whole shell glow amber from within. Scuttle inside for shelter.

They say the long-tailed-water-horse used to come by Ord twice a year to suck the whelk shells clean. I am breathing through tangles of fishing net. When I close my eyes the whole bed shakes. Let's go hunt for whelk shells.

The whelks drill holes in the shells of untrue whelks, dog whelks, mussels. They taste the water with their feet. My feet are forgotten, coiled in the damp sheet, clammy and unseen, trying for flippers.

The maidens of Ord used Dog whelks to dye cloth red. The maidens of Ord rode the back of the water horse secretly at night – red capes writhing behind. Come up the river and find me. Come up from the secret river that hides under the city. I remember sea air opening my lungs, iodine in my nostrils, spume foaming my hair.

The tissues have run out, my glass is empty, I've cut myself again on a blister pack. The bones of the water horse bleach on a garden wall and the whelk shell sits there on my bedroom shelf, fractal.

www.ingramcontent.com/pod-product-compliance
Lightning Source LLC
Chambersburg PA
CBHW011802040426

42449CB00017B/3471